TAPPING FEET

How Two Cultures Came Together to Make an American Dance

written by Moira Rose Donohue
illustrated by Colin Bootman

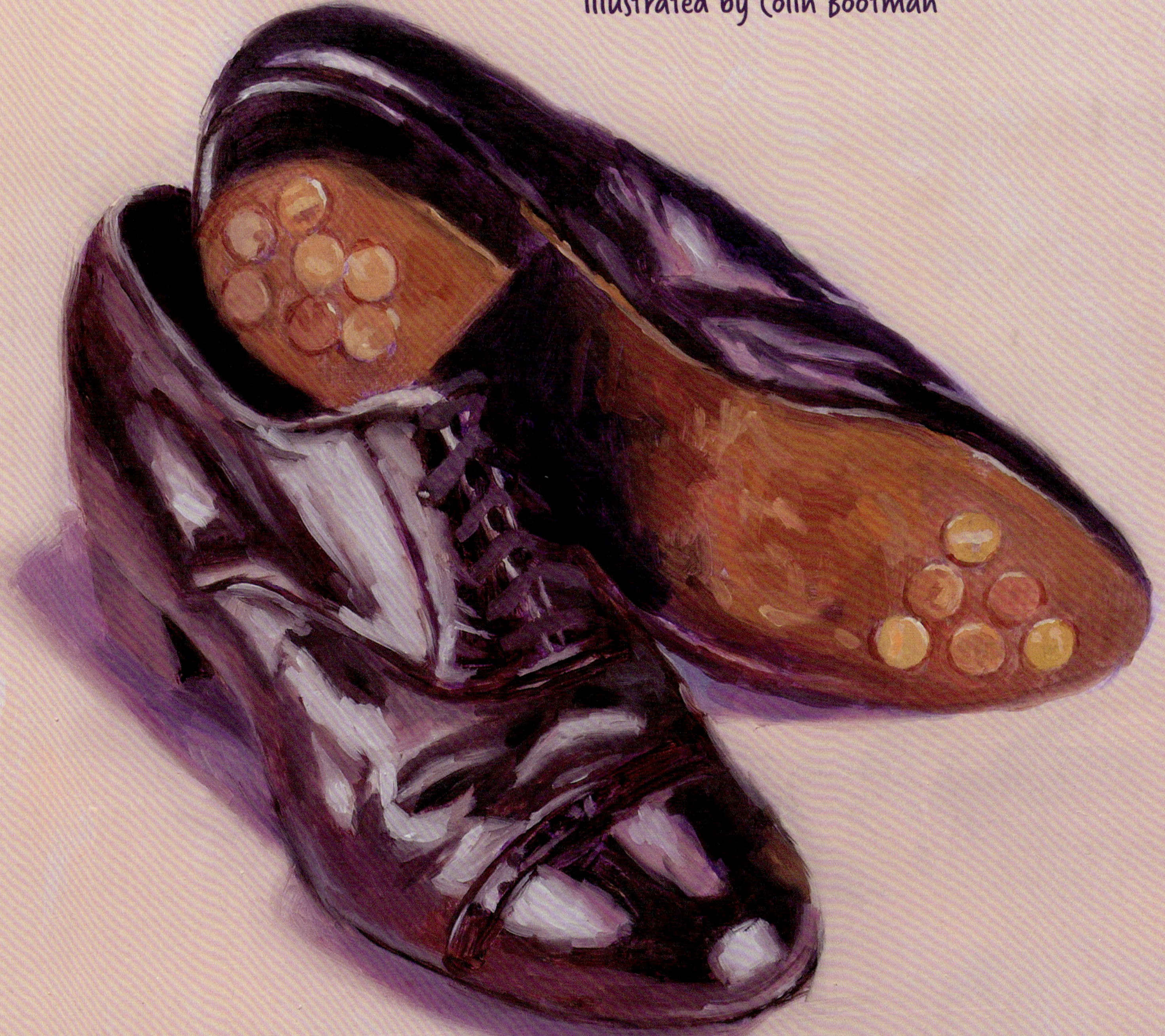

SLAP AND FLAP,
DOUBLE CLAP,
STEPPING IN A DANCE
CALLED TAP.

In the mid-1800s, famous British author Charles Dickens visited the lower east side of Manhattan in New York City. There, he watched a teenager spin on his heels, turn in his knees, and stamp his wooden-soled shoes. This was a dance unlike any he'd seen before. It was a new dance. An American dance. Tap dance.

This was a time in history when enslaved freedom seekers fled to New York City from Southern plantations to escape a terrible life of whips and chains. They were from families that had been taken from Africa against their will.

This was also a time when immigrants sailed there from Ireland to avoid starvation during the potato famine.

Their stories were different. But both groups of people had something in common—they weren't welcome.

And they had something else in common, too—
they loved to dance.

RHYTHM,
BEAT,

POUNDING FEET,
DANCING IN THE CITY STREET.

The people from Ireland—Irish Americans—danced by moving their feet quickly, keeping their arms and upper bodies stiff. This was an ancient form of Irish dance called a jig.

TOE AND HEEL,
JIG AND REEL,
IRISH DANCE WITH ARMS OF STEEL.

African Americans danced with loose arms, swaying like palms in the breeze, as they stomped their feet and slapped their thighs to make drum sounds. This type of dancing was called patting juba.

Buck and wing,
Feet that sing,
Spin and sway
with arms
that swing.

The two groups watched each other. Then they talked to each other. Finally, they borrowed steps from each other.

One dancer, African American William Henry Lane, watched more closely than the others. He copied some fast steps and kicks from Irish jigs and added them to African American body thumps, shuffles, and slides.

IN THE MIDDLE,
PARADIDDLE,
DANCING TO
THE FIERY FIDDLE.

Then he made up his own steps.

One day, Lane performed in Almack's Dance Hall in Five Points. Five Points was an overcrowded neighborhood in New York City. People from many countries had landed there.

In Five Points, there were as many cultures as spices in a stew.

The audience at Almack's loved Lane's grace, footwork, and lightning-fast pats. They called him Master Juba. Charles Dickens called him the "greatest dancer known."

But an Irish American named John "Jack" Diamond wasn't so sure. A few years before, he had won a city-wide jig contest. And he had performed in the dance halls as well.

JACK IS TOUGH.
TOE, HEEL, SCUFF.
IRISH JACK'S GOT
TAPS ENOUGH.

In 1844, Diamond challenged Lane to a dance competition later known as a "cutting" contest. Many people, including Jack himself, thought he could outdance Master Juba. Jack Diamond was good. But was he better?

Lane danced—a single shuffle, a double shuffle, a cut and cross-cut. Diamond was no match for him. Master Juba won!

DIG AND CRAMP,
STOMP AND STAMP,
MASTER JUBA'S
CROWNED THE CHAMP.

The two dancers took their competition on the road. For the next few years, they traveled around the country, competing night after night.

People flocked to theaters to see this new dance.

Sadly, both men died young. But their dancing lived on—in traveling stage shows and on Broadway, in shows created in the early 1900s by Irish American song-and-dance man George M. Cohan.

DANCING MAN
GEORGE COHAN,
OWNING BROADWAY IS HIS PLAN.

To make their steps louder, tap dancers nailed pennies, and later metal taps to the wooden bottoms of their shoes. They wanted to be heard.

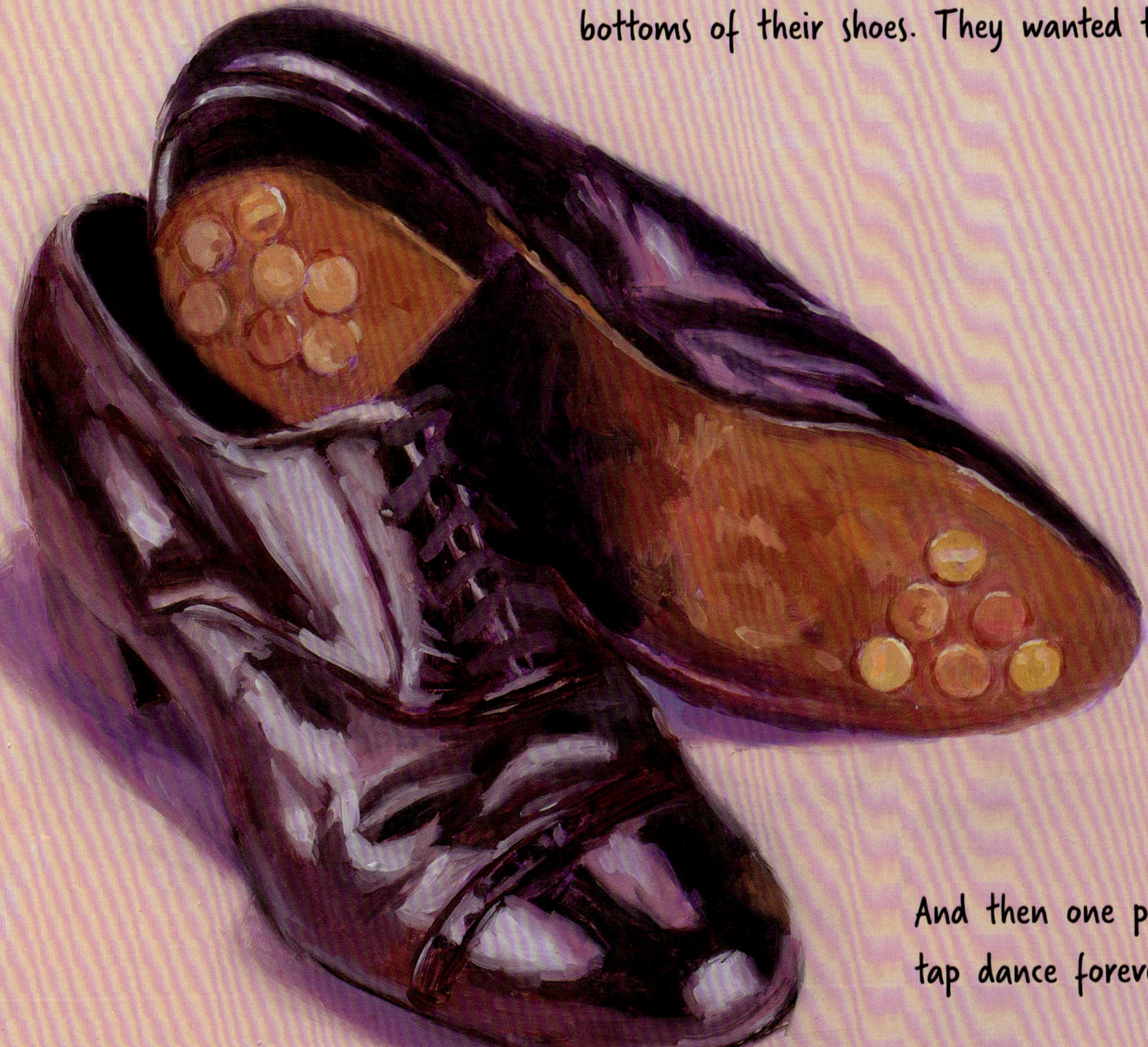

And then one person changed tap dance forever.

African American Bill "Bojangles" Robinson took Master Juba's dance steps and did them on his toes instead of flatfooted. In the 1930s, he danced in the new sound movies called "talkies." Moviegoers everywhere saw Bojangles take the hand of six-year-old Shirley Temple and dance up and down a staircase with her. Tap dancing took center stage!

BOUNCING HAIR,
SHIRLEY'S THERE
WHEN BOJANGLES
CLIMBS THE STAIR.

Over the years, tap dancers added their own style to the dance. The African American Nicholas Brothers danced in step with each other.

African American Clayton "Peg Leg" Bates tap danced with a wooden peg leg.

KNOCK ON WOOD,
PEG LEG'S GOOD,
ON TV AND HOLLYWOOD.

Irish American Gene Kelly added athletic and balletic moves to his dance.

And Fred Astaire and Ginger Rogers, who were neither Irish American nor African American, added tap steps to elegant ballroom dancing.

In the 1970s, newer dances became popular. Tap dancing was almost forgotten.

But in the 1980s, African American tap dancer Gregory Hines took to the wooden floor. He created fancier rhythms and made more sounds than an angry woodpecker.

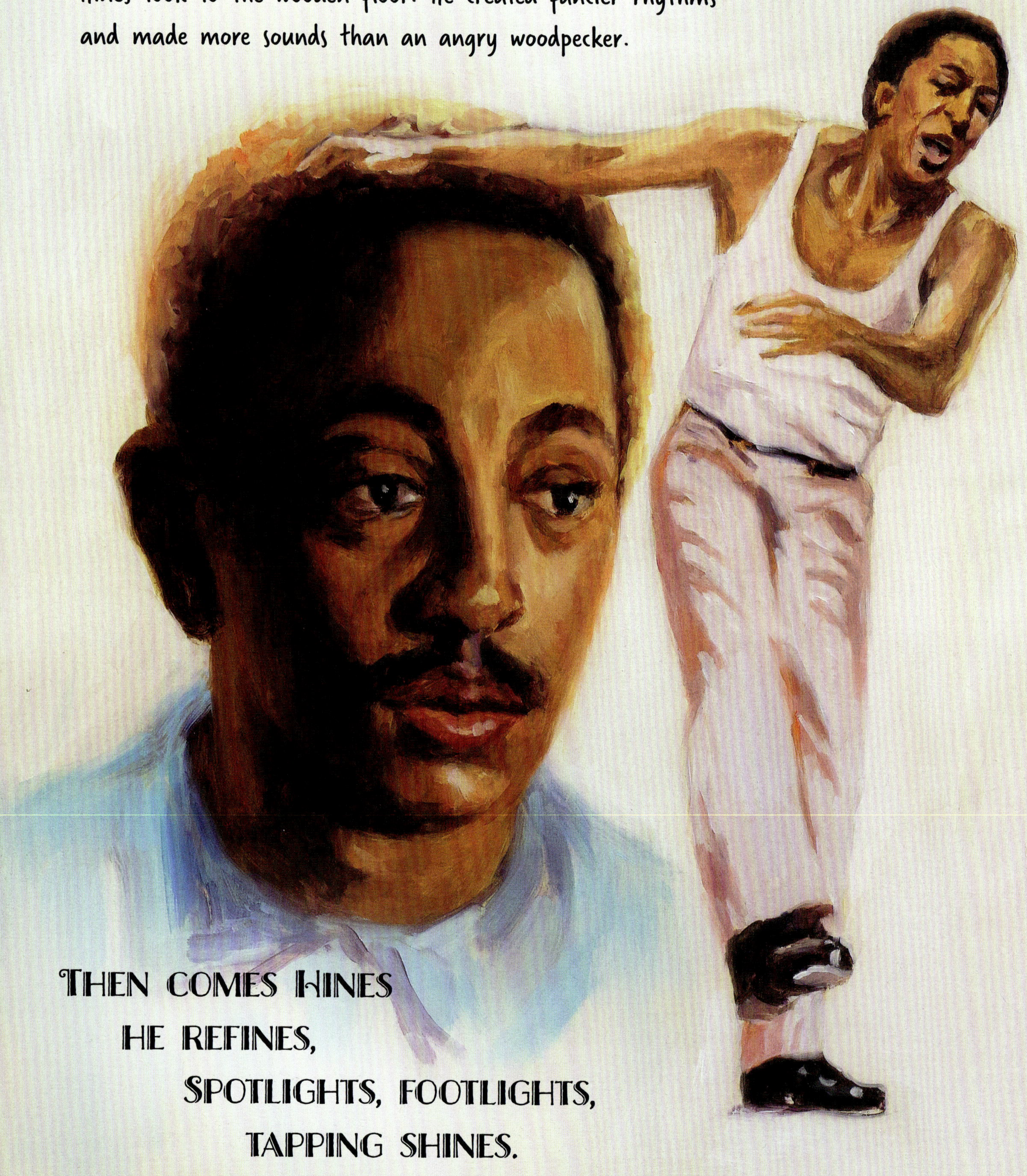

THEN COMES HINES
HE REFINES,
SPOTLIGHTS, FOOTLIGHTS,
TAPPING SHINES.

People wanted to dance like him. One person, Savion Glover, studied with him. Savion, The Tap Dance Kid on Broadway, made more noise and more funk as he danced with "Happy Feet."

The Five Points neighborhood has changed and has been renamed. The friendly relationship between the Irish Americans and the African Americans didn't last. But tap dance, created when two cultures came together for a moment in time, lives on in film, on Broadway, and in dance studios everywhere.

DANCE HIP-HOP,
DANCE TO POP,
BUT NEVER LET THE
TAPPING STOP!

WORTH ST

AUTHOR'S NOTE

While this true story of the origins of tap dance is a positive one, the two cultures involved have both faced terrible hardships that are not described in this book. Years ago, African people were taken, in chains, from their homes in Africa against their will. They were bought and sold, and enslaved by people living in America. To escape this misery, they ran away in the dark of night, hoping to reach states that didn't allow slavery. But sometimes, under the Fugitive Slave Act, they were returned if caught.

Irish immigrants from the mid-1800s, mostly Catholic, came from a country that, like the United States before the Revolution, was subject to British rule. They were not allowed to own the land on which they lived and were barely able to grow enough food to eat. When a terrible disease attacked their potato crops, more than one million people died from starvation. During that time, some fled to the United States. But once here, they could not find work. Businesses posted signs: "Irish Need Not Apply."

After Bill "Bojangles" Robinson, classic tap dance was preserved and performed primarily by African Americans. That's why when the United States Congress created National Tap Dance Day, it chose to celebrate it on Robinson's birthday, May 25. As an avid tap dancer and an Irish American born and raised in New York City, I celebrate it with a tap dance!